Original title:
Under the Cedar's Spell

Copyright © 2025 Creative Arts Management OÜ
All rights reserved.

Author: Mariana Leclair
ISBN HARDBACK: 978-1-80566-717-9
ISBN PAPERBACK: 978-1-80566-846-6

The Song of Soft Needles

In the shade where needles drop,
Squirrels dance and never stop.
Jumping high, they chase their tails,
While the birds share silly tales.

A ladybug takes the lead,
In this tree-top frolic creed.
Laughter rings from every bough,
As they gather for the show!

Enchantment in Every Needle's Fall

A tiny leaf on a giant tree,
Wonders if the wind is free.
It twirls like a dancer bright,
Laughs as it takes a flight.

The branches wave, a merry cheer,
As they whisper secrets near.
Each needle drops a giggly sound,
Nature's joy all around!

The Cedar's Cherished Apostles

The ants march on a sticky trail,
Dressed up for their daily gale.
Underneath the looming green,
They've got the best routine, it seems!

Mice play tag in the moonlight glow,
Holding tiny acorn shows.
Chirping frogs join in the fun,
Sporty leaps, their day is done!

Breath of the Green Giants

The breeze brings tales of old,
When the cedar trees were bold.
They chuckle at the clouds above,
Sharing wisdom wrapped in love.

Beneath their topsy-turvy limbs,
Frogs recite their woodland hymns.
Nature's party never ends,
With every breeze, a laugh it sends!

Lullabies in the Cedar's Embrace

In a grove where squirrels spin and twirl,
A raccoon juggles acorns with a swirl.
A frog croaks out a silly song,
As the drowsy leaves dance along.

Dreamy whispers float through the air,
While giggling foxes play without a care.
The nightingale sings, but it's off-key,
Bringing laughter to all, even the tree.

Mysteries of the Evergreen Sanctuary

Why did the pine tree wear a hat?
To keep its needles safe from the spats!
And the owl, wise with its silly glasses,
Hoo-hoos to the deer who stroll in classes.

Chipmunks ponder, 'What's for lunch?
A peanut or two? Or a nutty crunch?'
While the trees gossip about the elks,
They laugh so hard, they almost melt.

Beneath the Celestial Pines

Stars twinkle like berries on a vine,
As raccoons share a dance, feeling fine.
They wear tiny shoes, a mismatched pair,
While owls roll their eyes, but can't help but stare.

A squirrel claims it spotted a ghost,
But it's just a shadow he likes to boast.
A night full of giggles and dandy sights,
Harnessing joy as the moon shines bright.

Enchantment of the Woodland Air

In the woodland, where chatter never ends,
Each critter boasts about their wild trends.
A rabbit hops and tells a tall tale,
While beetles dance, waving their tiny veil.

The breeze carries laughter, soft and sweet,
As hedgehogs tumble on their little feet.
Together they share a merry refrain,
In the joyous realm where fun's never plain.

Enchanted by Woodland Shadows

In shady groves where squirrels squeak,
The mushrooms dance, oh so unique.
With acorns flying through the air,
The forest folk show little care.

A chipmunk prances, quite a sight,
He challenges a snail to a fight.
The owl hoots softly, laughs in jest,
While rabbits hold a hopping fest.

Forest Calls and Mystic Thralls

The trees conspire with leaves aflutter,
As raccoons giggle, getting to utter.
A fox tells tales of late-night runs,
Where shadows play and laughter stuns.

Beneath the boughs, a frog croaks loud,
Mimicking the whispers of the crowd.
While ferns engage in wild debates,
About which one of them is great.

The Green Veil of Hidden Whispers

In a glen where secrets collide,
Bumblebees buzz with undeniable pride.
A peacock struts in polka dot,
While doves argue who gets the spot.

A hedgehog dances, prickly but spry,
Claiming he can reach the sky.
While toadstools giggle at their own aim,
As if they didn't forget their name.

Timeless Tales from Bark and Leaf

The woods are alive with tales to spin,
Of owls that hoot and frogs that grin.
Each tree has a story, wait and see,
Told by the ants, with glee like tea.

A wandering breeze gives a gentle tease,
While trees sway lightly, bending with ease.
Each rustle in shadows, a giggling sound,
Where mischief and laughter can always be found.

In the Realm of Nature's Solace

In a grove where squirrels prance,
A dance-off starts, oh what a chance!
The birds chirp loudly, judging competitively,
While the doughnut thieves plot their next spree.

A rabbit hops with grace and flair,
His top hat on, he's quite the player.
Racquets and balls in the fun, they bring,
All laughing together, oh what joy they sing.

Amidst the trees, the shadows swing,
Grasshoppers cheer at each silly fling.
With every leap, they create new laws,
And the wise old owl just gives a pause.

Nature's laughter bounces on each breeze,
With the flora and fauna, all at ease.
Join the joyful romp, it's quite a sight,
In the realm, where humor takes flight.

The Crown of Green Dreams

Beneath the boughs, where shadows play,
A lizard struts in a quirky way.
Dressed in leaves as his royal gown,
He claims his throne without a frown.

Frogs in tuxedos sing opera notes,
While bees wear shades, buzzing like boats.
The flowers giggle, their colors bright,
As they sway along, full of delight.

A fox spins tales of brave exploits,
While raccoons plan late-night food fights.
With every giggle from the forest wide,
The jester squirrels break from their pride.

Through whispers and chuckles, joy starts to bloom,
The crown of green dreams dispels the gloom.
Join the revels, let troubles unlace,
In this kingdom of laughter, find your place.

Harmony in the Cedar's Nest

In a nest where mischief reigns supreme,
A chipmunk dreams of a birthday theme.
With cupcakes stacked, oh what a sight,
His pals arrive, ready to celebrate right!

The doves pop balloons, a colorful show,
While the hedgehogs roll cakes to and fro.
Each slice they share brings giggles galore,
As they're covered in icing, they all adore.

With a band of bugs playing cheerful tunes,
Dance breaks out beneath the bright moons.
Cedar branches sway to the rhythm divine,
Echoing laughter, a friendship so fine.

Harmony buzzes, it fills the air,
Nature's party—a whimsical affair.
So gather around, for it's truly the best,
In the embrace of life, we are blessed.

Secrets of the Silver Hour

As dusk drapes softly, shadows emerge,
The laughter of critters begins to surge.
A turtle shouts out jokes, full of wit,
While dancing fireflies put on a skit.

The moon peeks in with a whimsical grin,
As the owls tell tales of where they've been.
Frogs are croaking in perfect sync,
As squirrels plot pranks over a wink.

Under the stars, with a wink and a nod,
A raccoon strikes poses like a clod.
His friends roll around, unable to stand,
In the silver twilight, the fun is grand.

Secrets unfold as the night unwinds,
With all of nature sharing their finds.
Laughter and friendship roam the great skies,
In this hour of silver, where joy never dies.

Reflections in the Forest Pool

A squirrel made a splash, oh what a scene,
His acorn lost, his face quite serene.
Fish giggled softly, beneath the blue,
While birds chattered gossip, so loud and true.

A frog leaped in, and landed with flair,
Wearing a crown made of dandelion hair.
The sunset laughed, painted skies with gold,
As merry, tiny critters danced bold.

The Dance of Shadows in the Pines

Stillness begets a jitterbug show,
As shadows leap high, and then dip low.
The wind starts to whistle a cheeky tune,
While branches sway wildly, like dancers at noon.

A rabbit hops forward, not quite in sync,
His two left feet make the others rethink.
Yet laughter erupts, it's a comical sight,
In this forest of whimsy, under pale moonlight.

Unspoken Words in the Cedar's Heart

A chipmunk sat silent, all wrapped in thought,
Contemplating acorns that he never sought.
A deer quirked an eyebrow, her tail in a fling,
"Why so contemplative, let's dance and swing!"

The moon winked overhead, casting jokes with glee,
As shadows conversed about who climbs the tree.
With each silent giggle and rustling delight,
Nature twirled softly, igniting the night.

Threads of Life in the Evergreen Weave

In tangled branches, a tale unfurls,
Of owls in capes, doing twirls and swirls.
A raccoon with glasses reads a fine book,
While a pine cone chuckles, and gives him a look.

The moss forms a carpet for the ants' parade,
Each tiny foot tapping, music is made.
With laughter and chatter, the forest buzzes,
In this yarn of life, all nature just fusses.

Nature's Cryptic Archive

In the shadows, squirrels conspire,
With acorns as treasure, their fate's on fire.
Beneath the boughs, the mushrooms chat,
Debating tactics on how to combat.

The branches quirk and twist with glee,
As bees are buzzed like they're on spree.
A rabbit hops, wearing a crown,
Promising bread when the snail's in town.

The breeze tells tales of old, it seems,
Of ants who march with grander dreams.
While crickets tune their wild serenade,
Each leaf a page where nature parades.

So dive in deep, oh wanderer bold,
In this archive where secrets unfold.
The forest laughs, with leaves that snicker,
Whispers of mischief, a little slicker.

Magic Lurking in the Ferns

Fern fronds sway, in a dance, they prance,
With tiny fairies caught in their trance.
Mushrooms giggle, wearing tiny hats,
While frogs croak jokes, and converse with bats.

The wind carries whispers of bean curd pies,
As hedgehogs tune in to squirrel's lies.
Upon the rocks, a snail plays chess,
Decorating the board with a leafy mess.

Elves skitter 'round on mushroom tops,
Painting laughter while the bumblebee hops.
A dance of shadows bursts forth in light,
As owls drop puns, still up through the night.

So if you wander where shadows gleam,
Magic's not far, it's a giggling dream.
Stay for a pint of dew from the fern,
And share a laugh that takes a turn.

The Depth of Forest Whispers

In the depths where the shadows meet,
A tree declares itself quite a treat.
Whispers of laughter flutter about,
With raccoons plotting their nighttime rout.

Moss talks in riddles beneath a hat,
A sly little smile where critters sat.
The owls drop wisdom, or is it pride?
As wildflowers giggle, all side by side.

Crickets chirp with perfect timing,
While beetles roll dice, plotting and rhyming.
A fox makes plans for a prank on the hare,
With berries and giggles hidden everywhere.

So if you pause in the quiet glen,
Join the forest's old, jovial den.
Where laughter's the thread that binds each tale,
And each step forward makes giggles prevail.

Veils of Mist Amongst the Pines

Through veils of mist, the secrets collide,
Pine trees shuffle, misty-tongued guide.
A gnome hides treasure beneath the bark,
While shadows dance, igniting the dark.

Mice in tuxedos plan a grand show,
Piñatas of nuts that sway to and fro.
Whispers weave in the armchair of leaves,
As bees sum up what everyone believes.

A rabbit recounts the gear he misplaced,
Caught by the owl – with humor embraced.
The wind laughs softly, a tickle on cheek,
Muffling the jokes that the billy goat speaks.

Step lightly here, for who knows the score?
Among the pines, there's always much more.
With laughter as currency, it's clear to see,
Nature spins tales, forever carefree.

Revered Guardians of the Forest

The wise old trees all stand in line,
With leafy hats, looking so fine.
They gossip tales of squirrels and birds,
While spreading rumors through rustling words.

A chipmunk winks with a nut in cheek,
"Do you think the raccoons are playing hide and seek?"
The owls just hoot with a knowing grin,
"Keep it down, friends, the party's about to begin!"

Sunbeams dance on the forest floor,
While critters race for a snack to score.
The trees can't help but laugh so loud,
"Eat up, little ones, and make us proud!"

Beneath the boughs, mischief thrives,
Nature's jesters keep the joy alive.
In this leafy world, all are friends,
Where the laughter echoes and never ends.

Magic Found in Nature's Grove

Sprightly sprites with wings so bright,
Play peek-a-boo in the soft twilight.
A rabbit tells jokes, that's quite a treat,
While raccoons breakdance on their little feet.

"Got a carrot?" the rabbit says with glee,
But everyone's munching on wildberry brie!
The trees sway with rhythm, oh what a show,
While the brook sings along with a bubbly flow.

Mushrooms sport hats, in colors galore,
While critters tap dance on the forest floor.
"Step right up!" the hedgehog declares,
"The bravest ones can win silly dares!"

With laughter bubbling in the air,
Nature's secrets are laid bare.
Just follow the fun, let worries drift,
In the grove where wild wonders shift.

Beneath the Canopy of Wonder

A parrot squawks with tales absurd,
Of a cat that chased a fluffy bird.
The trees all chuckle, swaying high,
"Just watch the ground, and don't be shy!"

Dandelions giggle with fluffy dew,
"Why did the bee fly over you?"
The answer hangs in the morning air,
"Because the flowers could use some flair!"

A dance of shadows plays on the ground,
Where silly secrets abound all around.
The wind whispers jokes through the pines,
"Keep your paws off my lunch, or you'll pay fines!"

Time ticks slow in this enchanted place,
Where every critter wears a silly face.
In the canopy high, laughter takes flight,
Join the fun until the fall of night.

Enigmas in the Understory

In the underbrush, odd things appear,
Like mushrooms wearing hats of cheer.
Toadstools giggle as beetles parade,
In this wacky world of leafy charades.

A snail tells stories, slowly and grand,
Of adventures shaping this whimsical land.
"Why rush?" it smiles, "Life's a game!
Turn it upside down; nothing's ever the same!"

The bushes whisper tales of old,
Of daring deeds and adventures bold.
"Who's there?" calls a fox with a tilted head,
"Just the trees having fun," the rabbit said.

So gather, friends, in this riddle-filled nook,
Where laughter and joy replace every book.
Among the shadows, the stories run deep,
In nature's embrace, secrets we keep.

Beyond the Tranquil Limbs

In shady spots where critters cheer,
A squirrel danced to nature's beer.
His moves were grand, a sight to see,
    A furry jester, wild and free.

The rabbit laughed with joy and glee,
Not caring 'bout the buzzing bee.
He hopped around with quite the flair,
    Pulled off his best, ridiculous hair.

The breeze brought tales from faraway
Of silly squirrels and bold ballet.
With every gust, the stories spun,
Where laughter sparks and frolics run.

Beneath green limbs, the joy spread wide,
With each silly step, no need to hide.
For under branches, pure delight,
The woodland's charm ignites the night.

Serene Silence in the Woodland Realm

The owls hoot jokes in midnight's light,
Their punchlines land, it's quite a sight.
A raccoon snickers from the tree,
As leaves applaud, quite smug and free.

A bear in shades struts with a grin,
Each step he takes, a jig, a spin.
"Oh, it's my forest, watch me groove!"
The pine trees sway, they can't help but move.

The shadows chuckle; the stars blink twice,
As silent laughs roll like a dice.
No need for words, just gaze around,
In this woodland, joy is truly found.

As twilight fades, the critters rest,
Dreaming of puns and jesters blessed.
In silent laughter, bonds are tight,
Within this realm, all hearts take flight.

Cedar Dreams in Nature's Palate

A skunk spilled paint on snoozing fawn,
He woke with shock at the break of dawn.
With laughter bright, they made a scene,
Colorful tales where humor gleans.

The sparrows chirp in silly tones,
While lizards dance on ancient bones.
Each beetle struts with classic flair,
In this wild circus, naught a care.

The creek sings songs of playful pranks,
As chips of wood form rowdy flanks.
The trees shake hands with breezy grins,
While chubby chipmunks plot their wins.

Mirth fills the air like honey sweet,
Every critter shares a funny feat.
In this delight, laughter's our guide,
With nature's whimsy, joy's applied.

Caressed by the Evergreen Breeze

The wind whistles tunes through branches tall,
As critters join in a grand ol' ball.
A hedgehog twirls, his spikes askew,
With giggles spreading like morning dew.

The fox plays tag with shadows round,
While turtles trot through soft, warm ground.
Their laughter echoes, light and free,
Inviting joy from each green tree.

When ants parade in silly suits,
And grasshoppers wear tiny boots,
Nature chuckles, relishing fun,
In the dance of all, they're never done.

As evening falls and laughter swells,
The winds carry off our woodland spells.
Here beneath the starlit grove,
Silly hearts in nature's love.

Mesmerized by Needle and Bark

In the forest's embrace, we dance with glee,
Squirrels scold us for climbing their tree.
Branches sway, a whimsical show,
Twisting our laughter as we twirl to and fro.

Pine cones crash down, a comical plight,
Dodging them swiftly, what a silly sight.
The trees whisper secrets, giggles arise,
A forest of jesters, a prank in disguise.

Sunlight peeks through, a playful tease,
Tickling our noses with a savory breeze.
With needles for crowns, we march like a troop,
Claiming our kingdom, the whimsical group.

Laughter echoes, as shadows dance near,
A gathering of friends, full of good cheer.
Underneath branches where silliness reigns,
Life's just a caper, with laughter as gains.

A Retreat in the Forest's Heart

Leaves rustle softly, secrets abound,
In this leafy retreat, giggles resound.
Tangled in vines, we stumble and trip,
Nature's own slapstick, on this wild trip.

Mice play tag, while the owls just stare,
Wondering how we got tangled in hair.
Bushes are hiding our snacks, oh dear,
The chipmunks are laughing, it's all crystal clear.

Sunshine spills gold on our playful quest,
A treasure of fun, nature's own jest.
We build silly forts, with sticks and with leaves,
Imagination soaring, like the dance of the bees.

As twilight descends, our giggles ignite,
Chasing the fireflies, what a magical sight.
In this forest retreat, where joy finds its art,
We've found our own sanctuary, deep in the heart.

Serenity in Rustic Green

A blanket of moss, so soft and so grand,
Where squirrels wear hats and rabbits play band.
The old trees chuckle, they know every joke,
As shadows play tag with the wiggles and poke.

The wind hums a tune, so high and so sweet,
Drawing us in with its whimsical beat.
In the serenity, joy bounces around,
We frolic like children, no worries are found.

A dance with the daisies, a waltz with the ferns,
Caught in the laughter, our heartache adjourns.
Nature, a jester, with humor so light,
Turns our mundane moments into pure delight.

As butterflies flutter, our spirits take flight,
In this rustic green, we embrace the night.
Under branches that giggle, we find our release,
Wrapped in nature's laughter, we discover our peace.

Echoes of the Woodland Spirit

In the whispering woods, where giggles reside,
A spirit of mischief, our playful guide.
With stumps as our thrones, we rule with great flair,
A kingdom of laughter, with magic to spare.

Elves chuckle softly, their pranks well-timed,
In every rustling leaf, laughter's chimed.
We chase after shadows, caught in their game,
In the echoing woods, we're all quite the same.

Ricocheting laughter fills the serene air,
A symphony played by woodland's affair.
With critters around us, each moment a jest,
In the heart of the woods, we've found our own nest.

The stars start to twinkle, the night feels alive,
We gather our stories, the spirits derive.
Echoes of laughter, our treasure to keep,
In the wonder of woods, we happily leap.

Murmurs from the Green Abyss

In the shade where squirrels plead,
Ticklish leaves start to giggle.
A raccoon dons a crown of twigs,
Bears a grin, oh what a wriggle!

Amidst the mossy tales they tell,
A wobbly frog sings out of tune.
The wise old owl, with glasses wide,
Claims it's always past noon!

Dancing shadows prance and leap,
Grasshoppers join the joyful jest.
While wise trees chuckle deep in thought,
They've seen it all, they know best!

In giggly whispers, laughter swells,
Through branches reaching for the sky.
It's a party in this leafy realm,
Where fun and folly happily lie!

Guardians of the Enchanted Grove

Beneath a cloak of twisting vines,
Gnomes engage in cheeky tricks.
With jellybeans and giggle fests,
They throw nuts, watch how it clicks!

The bumblebees buzz with delight,
While grass blades play hide and seek.
A chubby badger makes a bow,
And claims he's quite unique!

Old pine yawns, its pinecone falls,
It lands right on a sleeping hare.
With a jump and flip, he hops away,
Glaring at the pine with flair!

These tiny guardians chant and cheer,
With laughter carried on the breeze.
In this enchanted, giggly nook,
Every day is filled with ease!

The Allure of the Evergreen Heart

Oh, the trees wear gowns of green,
Scruffy squirrels choose their dance.
While birds chirp in silly tones,
Reminds us of a rom-com chance.

With acorns sprinkled all around,
Chipmunks gather for a taste.
A fox in shades does a twirl,
As if life's a fun-filled waste!

Laughter rings through emerald halls,
As shadows tease like playful sprites.
The scent of pine, a magic spell,
Turns the world into delights!

In this forest, joy is ripe,
Where every leaf knows how to play.
An evergreen heart beats with cheer,
Making mundane days feel like a holiday!

Tales Carried on the Forest Wind

Through the woods, whispers flit around,
Of a squirrel's recent prank.
He replaced the nuts with candy corn,
And watched the birds give thanks!

Mice gossip in the moonlit glade,
Swapping tales of cheese and pie.
Each snicker bubbles like a brook,
Joining stars as they wink and sigh.

A bear who thought he'd known it all,
Danced with frogs in muddy shoes.
Now he's the king of wobbly fun,
In this forest, there's no excuse!

On the wind, laughter drifts and sways,
Between the trunks that smile and tease.
In this merry, wild enclave,
Life's a tune that's sure to please!

Secrets of the Coniferous Realm

In a forest so green, a secret's at play,
A squirrel in a suit leads the woodland ballet.
He spins with his acorns, a true little star,
While the chipmunks all chant, 'He's the best by far!'

The trees gently giggle, tickling the breeze,
As the fox in a top hat spins tales with such ease.
Laughter erupts from the critters nearby,
In this realm of the conifers, joy's never shy.

The owls in their glasses sip tea with a grin,
While the rabbits all dance wearing shoes made of tin.
They stomp and they hop, with much flair and delight,
Under branches where shadows play games day and night.

So join in the fun, let your worries all fly,
In a world where the branches tickle your sighs.
Here laughter's the rule, and silliness thrives,
Within this coniferous world, the heart truly jives.

Beneath the Boughs of Timeless Dreams

A bear with a beard, oh so fluffy and round,
Claims the best honey is best found underground.
He digs with a shovel—a ridiculous sight,
While the bees buzz around, all in giggles of flight.

The hedgehogs team up for a game of charades,
With costumes of leaves, and an owl masquerade.
Each whisper and chuckle ignites a wild cheer,
As branches sway softly, lending their ear.

A raccoon with a crown thinks he's king of the hill,
But slips on a pinecone, his throne gives a thrill.
The laughter erupts as he tumbles with grace,
A jester revealed in a royal disgrace.

Through the boughs, dreams float, dancing with glee,
In this wondrous wood where the fun's always free.
So wear your best giggle, don your joy like a beam,
And leap into wonders beneath the dream's gleam.

The Magic of Needle and Bark

In a grove where the needles form castles of green,
A rabbit finds magic in places unseen.
He offers a toast with a thimble of dew,
'Cheers to the fun, and to friendship, it's true!'

The pinecones have parties, with streamers galore,
Tiny ants do the dishes, while crickets encore.
From tall trees they giggle, their branches all sway,
As they dance through the night, in a magical way.

'Let's race to the stream!' calls a chipmunk with flair,
With his silly red cap and a tail in the air.
They tumble and trip over roots and some rocks,
Creating a symphony of giggles and knocks.

In this forest of laughter, with needle and bark,
Every leaf has a story, every shadow a spark.
With joy in the air and delight all around,
The magic of fun is where friendships abound.

Beneath the Whispering Canopy

Beneath branches that chatter and whisper aloud,
A parrot in glasses sings songs to the crowd.
His tunes are quite silly, they make the trees sway,
As the leaves burst with laughter, on this bright sunny day.

The raccoons hold meetings, discussing their heists,
But always end up sharing snacks and some advice.
With giggles and whispers, the forest is bright,
A community buzzing with joy and pure light.

A lizard in sandals strolls past with a grin,
He juggles three acorns, oh what a din!
Squirrels take bets on which one he'll drop,
As the canopy whispers; their spirits can't stop.

Beneath this vast ceiling where dreams intertwine,
Every critter delights as they sip on sweet wine.
So join in the mirth, let your troubles all flee,
For in this merry woodland, you're happy and free.

Under the Old Growth's Vigil

Amid the branches, squirrels dance,
Chasing shadows, they prance.
A woodpecker plays a gripping tune,
While mushrooms strut in the afternoon.

Woodwind whispers rustle leaves,
As playful spirits tease and weave.
A creature slips on acorn's dome,
Finding comedy far from home.

An owl hoots with sleepy glee,
While rabbits plot their jubilee.
From high above a crow takes flight,
Dropping twigs, oh what a sight!

In laughter's echo, joy takes hold,
Each tree a tale, each story bold.
Under the watch of nature's jest,
Life unfolds, a merry fest.

The Lore of the Fragrant Pines

In pine-scented air, tales are spun,
About critters having too much fun.
Beneath every branch, laughter swells,
As nature shares its quirky spells.

Chipmunks gather in a silly gang,
Playing pranks, oh how they clang!
A raccoon peeks from behind a tree,
Wearing a mask, as mischievous as can be.

The aroma of laughter fills the breeze,
While bees buzz by with utmost ease.
A gopher in shades, posing with pride,
Even the shyest critters can't hide.

With each wind's giggle, stories burst,
Of woodland frolics, ever reversed.
Beneath the pines where secrets lie,
All creatures' laughter fills the sky.

Beneath the Boughs' Gentle Touch

Beneath the boughs where shadows play,
A rabbit jokes about the day.
With a fine top hat and a grand bow,
He conjures the sun with a comic show.

A frog on a log sings off-key,
He jumps for joy, oh let it be!
Mud-smeared laughs in a peppy dance,
As butterflies waltz in a silly trance.

The gentle touch of branches sway,
Provides sturdy seats for antics at play.
With whispers of secrets and giggles galore,
Every critter bounces, who could ask for more?

Their uproarious tunes echo through time,
As laughter pokes through the forest's rhyme.
Beneath the boughs, all is absurd,
In their own world, not a soul disturbed.

Memories Caught in the Cedar's Gaze

Caught in a gaze where whimsy thrives,
Funny memories of woodland lives.
A bear with a hat tries to dance,
Tripping on roots, he doesn't stand a chance.

The whispers of leaves hold laughter dear,
Replaying moments year after year.
A hedgehog competes in a speedy race,
Rolling in place with a comical face.

Each branch holds tales of nature's cheer,
Where even the shy find the courage to steer.
A deer pokes fun at a sleeping fox,
While daylight fades, and evening knocks.

Within the twilight, joy remains,
Forest giggles wrapped in grains.
Caught in a gaze that never fades,
Where humor lingers in leafy glades.

Whispers of Evergreen Dreams

In the woods where squirrels play,
A gnome lost his way today.
He followed a squirrel's crazy dance,
Bumping into bushes, a clumsy chance.

The trees chuckled in leafy tones,
As he tripped over roots and stones.
With hat askew and face of glee,
He laughed at himself, wild and free.

Enchantment Beneath Boughs

A fairy with glittery wings,
Promised to grant all the best things.
But in her spells, she mixed up the tea,
Now toads are singing in harmony.

The rabbits are hopping, wearing hats,
As turtles teach them the latest dance stats.
They twirl under branches, what a sight,
With laughter echoing all through the night.

Shadows of the Ancient Arbor

The wise old owl perched on a limb,
Told stories of times that were quite grim.
But kids just giggled at his serious tone,
Creating wild tales of their own in fl tones.

Beneath the shadows, they spun a tale,
Of a giant snail on a quest to set sail.
With a map made of leaves, he'd roam the land,
And munch on daisies, oh how grand!

Beneath the Great Green Canopy

A raccoon in a mask searched for snacks,
While his friends wore hats and made fun of his tracks.
With every step, they had some fun,
Rolling in leaves, soaking up the sun.

But the canopy's whispers gave way to a shout,
As the raccoon fell and tangled about.
They all burst out laughing, what a big joke,
As he blushed under branches, the funniest bloke.

The Lure of Timeless Growth

In a forest where squirrels dance,
They wear little hats and take a chance.
With acorns thrown like party snacks,
The laughter echoes, never lacks.

The moss is plush, a leafy bed,
Where dreams are spun, with spice and dread.
A raccoon juggles pinecones high,
While chipmunks plot and giggle sly.

Sunlight filters through green hats,
Dodging the drips from maple spats.
The trees play tricks, get in the way,
As birds chirp jokes to start the day.

Songs of the Whispering Pines

The pines sing songs of breezy tales,
Of windy chases and snail trails.
Their needles echo silly tunes,
While gophers join the joyful croons.

A woodpecker's on a tapping spree,
Conducting all with glee, you see.
Each beat and peck, a drumline's cheer,
As critters gather 'round to hear.

The owls jest with rolling eyes,
While squirrels discuss their daring lies.
A banter floats, both rich and bright,
In the wood where laughter takes flight.

Harmony in the Fragrant Shade

In the grove where shadows play,
The daisies giggle, sway, and sway.
A lily pad sings lovely tunes,
As frogs recite their wacky prunes.

Butterflies dance with silly grace,
While grinning bees invade the space.
They buzz about, a choir sweet,
In nature's realm, none can defeat.

The scent of pine fills the air,
Mixed with sass from the lemon flare.
Squirrels debate, who gets the rest,
Of juicy berries, they jest and fest.

Enigma in the Cone's Shadow

Beneath a cone that hides a clue,
A raccoon wears a tutu, it's true.
He twirls and hops in evening glow,
While shadows whisper secrets low.

The mystery, who left the snack?
Was it a fox with tricks to pack?
The laughter roars through leafy lanes,
As creatures plot their weird campaigns.

In this place of curious dreams,
Things aren't always what it seems.
Pine cones grin with silly flair,
As night unfolds its comical air.

The Stillness of the Conifers' Gaze

In the shade where squirrels prance,
A lazy deer forgot to dance.
The pine trees yawn with every breeze,
And giggle softly at the bees.

The owls hoot jokes in ancient code,
While chipmunks debate their next road.
Branches sway, like dancers bold,
In this funny forest, tales unfold.

Underneath the needles' sway,
The bushes whisper, 'What a day!'
A funny scene, with laughter free,
Where even the roots join in with glee.

Nature's theater, wild and bright,
With every twist, a new delight.
In this grove, humor does reign,
As laughter echoes—oh, what a gain!

Legends Beneath the Green Veil

A tale of trees that wear their crowns,
With shakes and rattles, they share their frowns.
Legends sprout like mushrooms bold,
In the stories that these trees have told.

Laughter hides in every bark,
As branches dance, and shadows spark.
The wind will tease the leaves around,
As giggles whisper, without a sound.

The creatures plot their silly schemes,
To chase the marrow of their dreams.
In every nook, a jester waits,
To turn the myths to comic fates.

A world where laughter bends the boughs,
And wisdom wears a jester's blouse.
So heed the folktales of this land,
Where giggles grow like grains of sand.

Embracing the Celestial Canopy

Beneath the sky, the branches stretch,
The stars peek in, but they won't fetch.
The moon plays hide and seek with trees,
While mossy rocks crack jokes with ease.

The foliage twirls in playful cheer,
With every breeze, they tickle ear.
Night critters cackle, oh what a sight,
As bats join in and take to flight.

The constellations chuckle too,
As if they know a thing or two.
Astral humor in cosmic hues,
Laughter flows like radiant blues.

So dance beneath this leafy dome,
Find joy in telling trees your poem.
Embrace the night, let spirits dwell,
With stars and trees, all's well that's well!

The Myth of the Whispering Woods

In the heart of the woods, they say,
Trees gossip on a balmy day.
With rustling leaves, they share their news,
Of wayward birds and beaten shoes.

A woodpecker uses knock-knock jokes,
While raccoons sing, donning cloaks.
Silly sprites hide behind the trunks,
Making faces, full of funk.

The shadows dance, a partner brave,
As starlit paths the breezes pave.
Echoes twirl on the forest floor,
Unraveling giggles evermore.

So if you roam through this delight,
Stay tuned for laughs beneath the night.
The whispering wood might share a jest,
With chuckles, you'll surely be blessed.

Enchanted Roots of the Cedar Folk

In the woods where shadows dance,
Silly squirrels in woodland pants.
They juggle acorns, spin around,
While giggles echo, lost and found.

Mice throw tea parties on a stump,
With mushroom chairs, they bounce and jump.
The owls join in, wearing ties,
And share their tales beneath blue skies.

The raccoons hold a parade, oh dear,
With pots and pans, they bring good cheer.
Dancing shadows in the night,
All creatures join in pure delight.

Wandering gnomes, with hats so tall,
Play tricks on friends and sometimes fall.
As laughter swirls among the trees,
The night is filled with silly breeze.

Whispered Secrets of the Old Sentinel

There stands a tree with tales to tell,
Of sneaky pixies and all is well.
They whisper secrets, soft and sly,
As frogs in tuxedos hop right by.

Beneath its branches, shadows play,
As rabbits scheme their grand ballet.
With tiny hats and shoes of lace,
They leap and laugh in merry chase.

A fox, adorned in plaid design,
Offers punch in cups, divine.
While dancing fireflies keep the beat,
As woodland critters tap their feet.

Each evening brings a fresh charade,
A circus formed beneath the shade.
With goofy acts and silly rides,
In this grand show, no one hides.

Scented Reveries in the Moonlit Dusk

In twilight's glow, the laughter grows,
With lavender dreams and silly rhymes,
The skunks do waltzes, toes a-tap,
While chipmunks giggle in a heap with naps.

The hedgehogs roll in fragrant blooms,
As butterflies craft their fabric rooms.
With candy confetti filling the air,
They twirl and spin without a care.

Beneath the stars, the jokes take flight,
With comedic skits in the soft moonlight.
A bear wears glasses, acts all sage,
While raccoons dance upon the stage.

In this cherished realm where giggles lie,
Every creature gives it a try,
They sip on cider, munch on pie,
And under starlight, laughter flies.

The Voice of the Forest Spirit

A wisp calls out from leafy heights,
Where mischief lives in cozy sights.
A voice so gentle, makes them jump,
As turtles trumpet, thumping thump.

When shadows gather, pranks unfold,
With tales of treasures, bright and bold.
The llamas wear a jester's cap,
While beavers plot a tricky trap.

The spirit sings of ghostly fun,
As sunbeams glide, the day's now done.
A chorus of giggles fills the glade,
Where all the forest jokes are played.

Amidst this laughter, joy is found,
When critters leap with leaps profound.
With silly stories shared at will,
The forest whispers, "What a thrill!"

The Dance of Pine and Moonlight

In the night, the pines sway,
They cha-cha in a breezy ballet.
Moonlight giggles, sparks in the air,
As squirrels join the dance, without a care.

A fox jumps in, tiptoes and slips,
Tripping over roots with goofy flips.
Owls hoot their rhythm, wise and aloof,
While shadows jiggle, chasing a goof.

The branches laugh, a rustling glee,
As rabbits tap their furry feet with glee.
Stars wink above, sharing the fun,
In this crazy waltz, everyone's spun.

Who knew the woods had such flair?
When night falls, it's a wild affair!
The tall trees twist, swirl, and prance,
In a silly, starry moonlit dance.

Reverie in the Pine Needle Twilight

As twilight drapes the towering woods,
Little critters plot in the moods.
Cherry sap and pine cone hats,
Bears and bunnies chit-chat like chitchats.

A chipmunk juggles acorns with glee,
While the bees buzz in, sipping sweet tea.
Night rolls in and what a surprise,
Frogs start croaking, sharing their lies.

The fireflies wink like tricky friends,
Guarding secrets the forest tends.
With each flicker, a joke's been told,
In this enchanted grove, brave and bold.

Twilight laughs and the pine needles sway,
To the tune made by the woodland play.
Not a worry, just playful bliss,
In this twilight dance, all is amiss.

Stories Told by Ancient Roots

Beneath the earth, the roots conspire,
Weaving tales that never tire.
Whispers of the past in playful jest,
Reminding all of nature's quest.

Mole and mouse play charades anew,
While fireflies flash their best view.
The stories erupt from deep below,
Where laughter and mischief freely flow.

Each tree's a bard with branches spread,
Sharing secrets upon their head.
Owl rolls its eyes; it's heard it all,
Yet chuckles along, having a ball.

In this old grove, they frolic and cheer,
With every tale, they draw us near.
The roots may murmur, but hearts are light,
In a woodland of whimsy, pure delight.

Beneath the Swaying Limbs

Beneath the arms of ancient trees,
The forest giggles in the breezy tease.
Branches sway like they belong,
To a quirky tune, a silly song.

Raccoons wear masks, acting all sly,
Dancing around, oh my, oh my!
With the breeze as their partner, the leaves twirl,
Squirrels leap in, doing a whirl.

Laughter echoes from woodpeckers' taps,
As hedgehogs dream of grand mishaps.
The world's a stage where nature's wild,
A playground where every creature's a child.

With shadows leaping in the glade,
Every silly gesture, sweetly displayed.
Beneath swaying limbs, let spirits lift,
In this realm of laughter, a splendid gift.

Lost in the Beams of Sunlit Leaves

As I strayed beneath the green,
I tripped on roots, oh what a scene!
The sun peeked through, a wink, a jest,
I danced with shadows, feeling blessed.

A squirrel chuckled, high above,
With acorn jokes, it showed its love.
I shimmied left, then staggered right,
It's hard to walk when leaves invite.

A butterfly laughed, it twirled around,
While I tried to keep steady ground.
With every twist, I soon succumbed,
To leafy laughter, and I felt dumb.

Yet in this haze of leafy cheer,
I found a joy that felt quite clear.
And in the beams of sunlight's play,
I was the joke, and it was my day.

Reverie Amongst Timbered Giants

In the shade of giants, I did lay,
With whispers soft, they begged me stay.
Their trunks like towers, old and wise,
Yet I swear they giggled 'neath the skies.

A woodpecker knocked a silly tune,
Making the ponderous trees croon.
With each hard beat, they shook and swayed,
Even the moss seemed quite dismayed.

I pondered deep, what they would think,
As I spilled juice down my shirt—oh stink!
But the breeze just chuckled, cool and light,
These giants knew how to make things right.

Through swaying limbs, I caught that grin,
Their barky laughter pulled me in.
In timbered realms where dreams can soar,
I found that fun was worth much more.

Rooted in Earthly Wonder

With roots like fingers, deep in ground,
The trees conspired; oh what a sound!
They poked and prodded with leafy ears,
Whispering secrets mixed with cheers.

I looked around, bewildered, lost,
A patch of grass claimed my foot—I'm tossed!
The roots entangled like a playful game,
I laughed aloud; none felt the shame.

A wobbly gnome in the shade sat still,
His hat askew, like a crooked hill.
With leafy friends, he joined the jest,
Unlikely crew, but we felt blessed.

So here I twirled, a viney dance,
In muted giggles, I found my chance.
With every stumble, every blunder,
I reveled deep in earthly wonder.

The Spell of Swaying Branches

Beneath the branches, waving wide,
A lumberjack joked, then tried to hide.
A squirrel perched, its eyes agleam,
Swaying branches puffed like cream.

I tried to walk with graceful poise,
But tripped on twigs, oh such a noise!
The trees they chuckled, dressed in green,
As I danced stupid, a lovely scene.

A breeze came through, it took a bow,
Tickled my nose, oh I can't allow!
With every giggle, every twist,
I became part of the leafy mist.

So here I stay, with branches high,
Under their spell, I'll laugh and sigh.
In nature's realm, with joy transferred,
The spell of sway is felt, preferred.

Whispers of the Timeless Woods

In the forest, squirrels dance,
Chasing bugs, they take a chance.
Branches sway in cheerful glee,
Laughing at a bumblebee.

Mossy carpets, soft and neat,
Hiding where the shadows meet.
Trees with faces, oh so wise,
Rolling up their ancient eyes.

Frogs wear tuxedos, very fine,
Croaking jokes with perfect line.
Whispers float on breezy air,
Tickling noses everywhere.

In this realm of joyous cheer,
Nature sings, so loud and clear.
Each leaf rustles with delight,
As daylight fades, it's party night.

The Cedar's Embrace at Dusk

As the sun dips low and shy,
Fireflies blink a matchless hi.
Cedar branches make a stage,
For a squirrel in silent rage.

He's rehearsing his great play,
Falling nuts, a grand display.
Raccoons laugh, they can't resist,
Joining in the nutty twist.

Moonlight spills on leafy beds,
Bats invade with tiny heads.
Wombats wear their finest hats,
Drawing maps with silly spats.

Tickle fights with playful winds,
Whispers shared by furry friends.
In this grove, the night begins,
With giggles, chirps, and silly grins.

Spirit of the Ancient Trunks

In a forest thick and wise,
Woodpeckers tap in bold disguise.
Each thud brings a joke anew,
Echoes bouncing, laughter too.

Mossy giants stand so tall,
Telling secrets to us all.
Gnarled roots with wiggly tales,
Bringing smiles like feathered sails.

Owls wear glasses, looking smart,
Debating where the moonlight starts.
They plot the path of shooting stars,
While raccoons steal their candy bars.

Among the trunks, the spirits play,
Launching pranks at end of day.
Every tree's a giggle's source,
In this land, a joyful force.

Symphony of Forest Echoes

Nature's orchestra takes its place,
Chirping crickets lead the race.
All the critters join the band,
Playing tunes in an endless land.

Leaves are clapping, branches sway,
Frogs in hats take center stage.
Butterflies waltz in giddy flight,
While owls hoot jokes that feel just right.

A deer in sneakers takes a leap,
Chasing shadows, feeling deep.
Mice on ice skates glide and twirl,
Creating chaos, such a whirl.

As dusk falls, the music grows,
Singing praise to all that flows.
In this harmony of fun,
Every heartbeat beats as one.

Guardian of the Leafy Canopy

In the shade where squirrels play,
I spy a chipmunk rather gay.
He wears a hat, a tiny crown,
And dances around in his leafy gown.

The raccoons throw a picnic spread,
With acorns piled on a tiny bed.
They laugh and chatter, munching their feast,
While a rogue squirrel steals, to say the least!

A bird sings off-key, a bit out of tune,
As a frog joins in, croaking by noon.
Together they make quite the sound,
In this leafy realm where fun abounds.

Each rustle and giggle fills the air,
Nature's own stand-up, everywhere!
So here beneath the leafy spree,
We're guardians of a giggling tree!

Boughs That Hold the Sky

Tall and broad, they stretch so wide,
With owls in corners and birds with pride.
If you listen close, you might just find,
A gossiping breeze that's one of a kind.

The branches sway like they're on a date,
While shadows dance, oh, isn't it great!
A butterfly slips, in a slip-up quite grand,
Landing on a bear's outstretched hand!

The sun peeks through, a winking ray,
As ants march on with a crumb ballet.
Chasing each other like friends at play,
A bustle of fun in the boughs today.

All under the sky, in laughter we soar,
Even the pine cones tumble and roar!
With giggles and grins, we bounce on by,
In this treetop realm where the heart is nigh.

Tales from the Cedar's Heart

Once a chipmunk found a sock,
He wore it proudly, quite the shock!
Strutting around with fashionable flair,
While all his friends just stopped to stare.

The cedar whispered stories of old,
Of lovesick frogs who were brave and bold.
One jumped too high, and oh what a scene,
Landed right on a grumpy raccoon queen!

The winds carry chuckles, the leaves join in,
As laughter erupts from the smallest fin.
A mockingbird jests at a bug on a twig,
Singing the praises of humor so big!

So come gather 'round, let's spin a new tale,
Of furry shenanigans and winds that prevail.
For deep in the heart where the funny resides,
Lies joy and mischief in nature's divides!

Embracing the Green Enchantment

In the green, where mischief thrives,
A frog leads a dance, oh how he strives!
With a lily pad hat and a splashy boot,
He twirls and leaps, such a comical hoot!

A worm dressed up for a fancy ball,
In a ruddy coat that nearly made him fall.
He wobbled quite stiff, to his own piano,
While the ants took bets on his grand finale, oh!

The sunbeams giggle, tickling the grass,
As shadows whisper, letting time pass.
Each leaf is a witness to giggles and cheer,
In this enchanted grove, laughter is near.

So join in the fun, let your spirit sprout,
As the green magic twirls, there's no doubt!
With joy all around, let's jump and play,
In this merry land where the silly ballet!

Dreams Woven in Wood and Sky

In the shade where laughter grows,
Squirrels gather in tiny prose.
They gossip on acorn thrones,
And dance like kings on their wooden bones.

A breeze pulls pranks with a gentle nudge,
As leaves perform a funny judge.
Invisible hands tickle our toes,
While birds compose silly little shows.

The branches bend with a joking tune,
As shadows play beneath the moon.
Whispers linger in playful jest,
Nature's humor, truly the best!

In dreamland, trees wear capes so bright,
Imaginations take flight each night.
We laugh and wiggle, feel no dread,
As silly stories fill our heads.

The Spirit of the Cedar Forest

In a forest where chuckles blend,
The tall trees are our closest friends.
They lean in close, with boughs so wide,
Whispering jokes we can't abide.

A woodpecker laughs at a bad pun,
He's the jester when day is done.
While rabbits chuckle at his plight,
Cedar spirits join in the light.

We lounge on the grass, sense the fun,
As critters play 'til the day is done.
The forest giggles with every sound,
A symphony of joy that's profound.

Frogs croak out ballads with flair so grand,
Their rhythm keeps us hand in hand.
In the heart of the woods, we find our glee,
Where laughter flows like a wild sea.

Echoes of the Evergreen Thicket

In the thicket where wonders bloom,
Critters frolic, dispelling gloom.
Echoes bounce with joyous cheer,
A cacophony for all to hear.

Foxes wear masks, they play pretend,
While birds crack jokes without an end.
The pinecones giggle like little kids,
With secret tales that nature bids.

A raccoon, wise with a hint of sass,
Forages treasures in the grass.
He shares his finds with a wink so sly,
Crafting legends that soar up high.

The thicket shimmers with laughter bright,
As shadows dance in the soft moonlight.
Every creature joins in the jest,
Making the woods feel truly blessed.

Aroma of Nature's Serpent

In the forest where scents arise,
Snakes slither with mischievous eyes.
Their scales glisten as they play,
Leaving trails of laughter along the way.

A fragrant breeze brings tales untold,
Of sly tricks and jokes so bold.
The bushes rustle, concealing mirth,
As creatures blend with the earthy birth.

Worms tell tales of what they munch,
Their stories making us laugh a bunch.
With curls and twists, they spin the yarn,
A delightful mix of wood and barn.

The roots shake hands with the ground so firm,
Sharing whispers and giggles that squirm.
In every scent, a chuckle hides,
Nature's serpent in joyous rides.

The Dance of the Oldest Trees

In the forest, trees sway with glee,
Their branches dangle, quite carefree.
Squirrels giggle, and birds all cheer,
As the trunks boogie, year after year.

Roots twist and turn in a merry round,
While mushrooms laugh at the sight they found.
The oak wears glasses, the pine a hat,
Together they throw a tree-top spat.

They shuffle their bark, a comical sight,
The willows waltz, it's pure delight.
With every creak, a joke's been told,
As the forest busts out with laughter bold.

And as the sun dips low in the sky,
The trees take a bow, oh my, oh my!
With roots in the air and twigs in a swirl,
The oldest dancers in a leafy whirl.

Secrets Woven in Leaves

Leaves whisper tales in the breezy air,
Of acorns that tricked a wandering bear.
They giggle and chatter, secrets so sly,
About pinecones that plotted to fly high.

One leaf claims it once dated a twig,
While another declares, 'I'm quite the big fig!'
They rustle at night with stories galore,
Of shadows that dance and laugh by the door.

A squirrel sneezes, and leaves all dive,
'Bless you!' they cry, 'You're so live and thrive!'
With every gust, a new joke is spun,
These leafy companions know how to have fun!

The sun filters through with a chuckle and grin,
While roots below join in the din.
In this leafy realm, silly tales bloom,
As nature's own jesters brighten the gloom.

Whispers Beneath the Evergreen Canopy

Beneath the boughs of whispering trees,
The critters gather, feeling the breeze.
A hedgehog tries to tell a wise thing,
But fumbles it up, what a funny fling!

A robin chortles, 'Don't take a fall!'
As acorns roll down in a clattering ball.
The ferns wave their fronds in a playful rush,
It's a game of tag, and oh, what a hush!

In the evergreen shade, mischief unfolds,
Bunny hops high, his stories retold.
With each little giggle and silly surprise,
The humor outshines the sun in the skies.

And as evening descends with a flickering gleam,
The laughter of nature becomes dreamlike theme.
Under this canopy, the world's a delight,
Where every creature finds joy in the night.

Enchanted Shadows of the Ancient Grove

In the shadows of trees that are ancient and wise,
The giggles of critters reach up to the skies.
A mouse in a cloak with a hat so tall,
Claims he's the king of this leafy hall!

The owls hoot loudly, with laughter and cheer,
'The night is our stage, oh what a sphere!'
With shadows like dancers who flit and fly,
They trip on their branches, oh my, oh my!

The branches are curtains for shows that delight,
With fireflies flickering like stars in the night.
They croon the sweet tales of foolish care,
Where the tall, twisty trees all claim their share.

As the moon peeks through with a glimmering smile,
The grove comes alive, oh stay for a while!
With laughter and shadows, this enchantment grows,
In the heart of the forest where humor just flows.

Dance of the Hidden Spirits

In the grove where shadows play,
Little elves spin night away.
They trip and tumble, laugh and cheer,
Whisper secrets loud enough to hear.

With twirling leaves and giggling breeze,
They pull the squirrels from the trees.
Bouncing mushrooms start to sway,
Join the dance at the end of day.

The owls hoot out a funky beat,
While rabbits tap their furry feet.
A clamoring chorus fills the air,
As nature's revelers don't have a care.

So if you wander past the brook,
You might just catch a curious look.
From joyful sprites with mischief lighter,
In the night, the fun grows brighter.

Nature's Gentle Incantation

The sun beams down with cheeky smile,
As critters play and stop awhile.
A squirrel sipping from a cup,
While bees buzz by and won't give up.

The flowers sway in silly prance,
Inviting all for a funny dance.
A turtle dons a party hat,
While frogs leap high, oh imagine that!

The breeze seems to giggle, can't you hear?
It's nature's laugh that brings you near.
When leaves start ruffling just for fun,
You know the woodland's just begun.

So join the laugh; don't miss a bite,
For life in nature feels just right.
With every step, a chuckle grew,
In the gentle arms of morning dew.

The Forest's Gentle Caress

The branches wave, a soft hello,
As the shadows dance to and fro.
A raccoon wearing socks so bright,
Chases fireflies into the night.

Mossy carpets cushion the glee,
While nuts roll down—oh, what a spree!
A group of rabbits, painted in zest,
Hopping high, they claim their quest.

As sunlight filters through the leaves,
Even grumpy owls find reasons to tease.
They chuckle low and blink once or twice,
At the antics of creatures so nice.

In this land of giggles and quirky sights,
Every corner holds laughter and delights.
So wander here, let joy profess,
In the gentle woods, find happiness.

Soft Murmurs from Age-Old Trees

Whispering winds come out to play,
With stories spun in a funny way.
The trees chuckle with leaves so green,
Sharing secrets few have seen.

An old oak grins, a wise old sage,
Commands respect yet knows a page.
He tells of squirrels that dashed too fast,
And of silly bromances that never last.

The pines conspire, their needles tease,
With every rustle, they aim to please.
They drop their seeds with a wink and nod,
Hoping for pranks to keep them awed.

As dusk enfolds the laughter tight,
The woods erupt in pure delight.
For every rustling, every jest,
Is nature's call to simply rest.

The Pulse of the Forest Floor

In the woods where the squirrels play,
I tripped on a root, then cried 'Hooray!'
A dance of leaves was my only cheer,
As the owls hooted, I shared my fear.

The ground a bouncer, lifting my feet,
Flowers giggled, 'Oh, what a feat!'
A rabbit winked, said, 'Join the game!'
I fell again, but I felt no shame.

The mushrooms chuckled, quite in delight,
As I leaped for joy, aiming for flight.
But gravity laughed, and I hit the moss,
And nature sighed, 'Well, that's your loss!'

Yet laughter echoed through trunks so wide,
With every tumble, my joy couldn't hide.
So come, oh friends, let's have some fun,
For the forest floor gives joy to everyone.

Cedar Shadows on a Starlit Night

Beneath the stars, the branches creak,
I whispered a joke, the tree gave a squeak.
The moon grinned down, its face full of glee,
As shadows danced with a cheeky spree.

Crickets chimed in, their voices a buzz,
They played a tune with the softest fuzz.
I tried to sing, but the owls took flight,
Saying my pitch was a frightful sight!

The stars rolled their eyes, a cosmic jest,
As I twirled around, giving it my best.
The whispering cedars joined the charade,
In a hilariously leafy parade.

So here's to the shadows that dance in the night,
With laughter so bright, it sparks pure delight.
Underneath such stars, we find our own fun,
In cedar embrace, till the night is done.

Harmonies in the Whispering Pines

In the pines, a secret band,
With squirrels strumming, oh so grand!
They've formed a club for midnight tunes,
With bops and boops that shake the moons.

A woodpecker hopped in, a drummer true,
While raccoons joined in, the dance crew too.
We formed a line, our moves so slick,
But one fell down, now that was quick!

The pines all swayed, their needles a-green,
As nature laughed, it was quite the scene.
Our melodies echoed, a comical blast,
With critters giggling, the fun unsurpassed.

So, join the show beneath the trees,
Where laughter rings with the gentlest breeze.
In the pines, we'll sing till dawn light,
Making memories, our hearts take flight.

Beneath the Elfin Canopy

In a grove where the elves play tricks with ease,
I found my shoe tangled in giddy trees.
Leaves tossed confetti, oh what a scene,
As I danced round like a wobbly machine!

The fairies giggled, examined my plight,
While mushrooms plotted till well past the night.
A gnome told a tale, so silly and wild,
About how he'd once tamed a giggling child.

Beneath all the branches, the laughter went round,
With each little stumble, more joy to be found.
They served up nuts in the fanciest bowls,
While I shared my sandwich, which filled up their souls!

In this blissful nook where the magic unfurls,
Life's quirky dance is a gift to the world.
So come join the fun where the elves like to play,
In the elfin lands, let's laugh the night away!

www.ingramcontent.com/pod-product-compliance
Lightning Source LLC
Chambersburg PA
CBHW072147200426
43209CB00051B/821